AND THEN COME THE NIGHTJARS

BEA ROBERTS

And Then Come The Nightjars won the Theatre503 Playwriting Award 2014
and was developed and produced by Theatre503 and Bristol Old Vic.

It received its world premiere at Theatre503 in September 2015
before transferring to Bristol Old Vic.

AND THEN COME THE NIGHTJARS
BY BEA ROBERTS

CAST

Michael	David Fielder
Jeff	Nigel Hastings

CREATIVE TEAM

Director	Paul Robinson
Designer	Max Dorey
Lighting Designer	Sally Ferguson
Composer	Olly Fox
Sound Designer	Max Perryment
Casting Director	Matthew Dewsbury
Assistant Director	Rebecca Loudon
Assistant Designer	Daisy Young
Costume Supervisor	Ellen Bean

PRODUCTION TEAM

Producer	Jessica Campbell
General Manager	Jeremy Woodhouse
Associate Producer	Franky Green
Production Manager	Heather Doole
Stage Manager (London)	Lisa Cochrane
Stage Manager (Bristol)	Benedict Jones
Production PR	Chloé Nelkin Consulting
Resident Assistant Producers	Yasmin Joseph and Ceri Lothian
Literary Producer (Bristol Old Vic)	Sharon Clark

CAST

DAVID FIELDER (Michael)

David comes from a small cotton town in Lancashire called Todmorden. He trained in London at the Central School in 1970 and since then has performed over 500 roles in the UK and around the world, including spending several seasons with the Royal Shakespeare Company in Stratford-upon-Avon. He won the Manchester Evening News Award for his performance as Vladimir in *Waiting for Godot* at the Library Theatre, and Shylock in *The Merchant of Venice* at the Bolton Octagon Theatre. He recently returned from performing in *Hamlet* at the Gdansk Shakespeare Festival and will be performing excerpts from Beckett's novel *Company* with the music of Phillip Glass at the Manchester Literary Festival in October.

NIGEL HASTINGS (Jeff)

Nigel trained at LAMDA. His theatre credits include: *What Falls Apart* (Live Theatre); *Henry VI*, *Othello* (Shakespeare's Globe); *Hitchcock Blonde* (Hull Truck); *Gravity*, *Pravda* (Birmingham Rep); *Journey's End* (Duke of York's); *Animal Farm*, *The Lemon Princess*, *The Lady in the Van* (West Yorkshire Playhouse); *Gone* (New Ambassadors); *The Ugly One* (Theatre Royal, Norwich); *Amadeus* (Crucible, Sheffield); *Present Laughter* (Theatre Royal Bath); *Hurts Given and Received*, *Found in the Ground*, *The Fence* (Wrestling School); *Roundelay*, *Parting Shots* (Stephen Joseph Theatre); *Kindertransport* (Vaudeville); *Jerusalem Syndrome* (Soho); *All My Sons* (Theatre Royal Plymouth); *Twelfth Night* (Edinburgh Lyceum); *The Devils* (Theatr Clwyd); *As You Like It*, *A Midsummer Night's Dream* (Regent's Park); *Pride and Prejudice* (Manchester Royal Exchange).

Film and television includes: *Hanna's War*, *Hostage*, *Four Weddings and a Funeral*, *The Unbeatables*, *Peaky Blinders*, *The Shadow Line*, *Hustle*, *Rosemary and Thyme*, *Wire in the Blood*, *The Government Inspector*, *The Commander*, *A Touch of Frost*, *Cadfael*, *Soldier Soldier*, *The Big Battalions*, *A Bit of a Do*.

CREATIVES

BEA ROBERTS (Writer)
Bea Roberts is a West Country writer who grew up in a variety of pretty but oddly named villages on the periphery of Dartmoor.

Credits include: *Infinity Pool; A Modern Retelling of Madame Bovary* (Tobacco Factory Theatres/The Bike Shed Theatre/Plymouth Theatre Royal); *Scoop* (Lyric Hammersmith/UK tour) and *Nights with Dolly Henderson* (Box of Tricks at the Salisbury Playhouse/The Bike Shed Theatre/Bolton Octagon).

In addition to writing plays, Bea has written and performed sketches, storytelling pieces and stand-up comedy. She currently has work in development with Up In Arms, Pins and Needles Productions, the Bush Theatre and BBC Comedy.

PAUL ROBINSON (Director)
Paul is Artistic Director of Theatre503. His recent productions of *A Handful of Stars* and *Land of Our Fathers* both transferred to Trafalgar Studios and received four- and five-star reviews in the *Guardian*, *The Times*, *Independent*, *Telegraph* and *Time Out* and a total of nine OffWestEnd award nominations including Best Director.

He is a fervent advocate of new writing and has developed new plays at many of the country's leading theatres. Having graduated from the Bristol Old Vic Theatre School, he received an Arts Council Bursary to the Manchester Royal Exchange. He was selected to attend the National Theatre's Advanced Directors' Course and was a Staff Director at the National Theatre for three years.

For Theatre503: *And Then Come The Nightjars, A Handful of Stars, Land of Our Fathers, The Life of Stuff, Desolate Heaven, Life for Beginners, The Swallowing Dark, Salt Meets Wound, They Have Oak Trees In North Carolina* (Theatre503/Radio4), *The Lifesavers* (Colchester/TMA Award nomination), *Manor House* (Latitude Festival), *Porn: The Musical* (Best New Musical Award, The Offies), *Epic* (Latitude Festival) and *The Charming Man* (Best Director nomination, The Offies).

Other theatre credits include: *Big Sean, Mikey and Me* (Pleasance, Edinburgh); *Falstaff* (Cottesloe/Platform); *Duck Variations* (Olivier/Platform); *Hello and Goodbye* (ETT/Trafalgar Studios); *Breakfast with Mugabe* (Ustinov Bath Theatre Royal); *Who Killed Mr Drum?* (Riverside Studios); *World's End* (Pleasance/Trafalgar Studios) and the West End transfer of Tom Stoppard's *Rock 'n' Roll*.

MAX DOREY (Designer)

Max was the trainee designer at the Royal Shakespeare Company in 2013/14 and trained at the Bristol Old Vic Theatre School. He was a finalist for the Linbury Prize for Stage Design in 2013, and nominated for Best Set Design in the OffWestEnd Awards in 2012 and 2013.

Set and costume design includes: *Orson's Shadow, Teddy* (Southwark Playhouse); *Lardo, Marching on Together* (Old Red Lion); *Animals* (Theatre503); *Coolatully, Black Jesus* (Finborough); *Sleight and Hand* (HiBrow Productions/ BBC iPlayer, Summerhall Edinburgh); *I Can Hear You, This is Not an Exit* (RSC/ Royal Court Upstairs); *The Duke in Darkness, Marguerite* (Tabard); *Disco Pigs* (Tristan Bates/Alma Tavern); *The Good Soul of Szechuan* (Bristol Old Vic Studio).

Production design includes: *Standing Still, Anthony and Cleopatra trailer, Henry IV trailer, Richard II Live trailer, Arden of Faversham trailer* (RSC/ Dusthouse Films).

Puppet making includes: *Peter Pan* (Bristol Old Vic); *Cinderella* (Tobacco Factory); *Phaedra's Love* (NSDF).

SALLY FERGUSON (Lighting Designer)

Sally trained in Design for Performance at the Wimbledon School of Art. She works as a Lighting Designer across multiple disciplines including opera, dance, events and installations and is one third of Paper/Scissor/Stone Theatre Company.

Theatre credits include: *Shiver, Lost in Yonkers* (Watford Palace Theatre); *As You Like It* (Southwark Playhouse, co-design); *Microcosm, The Girl With the Iron Claws, Hag* (Soho); *Floyd Collins* (Southwark Playhouse); *The Sleeping Beauties* (Sherman Cymru); *Many Moons* (Theatre503); *Medea* (Platform Theatre); *The Marriage of Figaro* (Wilton's Music Hall); *Così fan tutte* (Village Underground); *Slowly* (Hammersmith Riverside Studios); *Trying* (Finborough).

OLLY FOX (Composer)

Olly is a composer, musician and teacher. He studied Drama at Manchester University and Music Design for Film and Television at Bournemouth University.

Theatre credits includes: *Blasted, The Pride, That Face* (Sheffield Theatres); *Dido, Queen of Carthage* (Sam Wanamaker Playhouse); *The Comedy of Errors, Macbeth, The Globe Mysteries, As You Like It, Bedlam, Troilus and Cressida, The Frontline, A Midsummer Night's Dream* (Shakespeare's Globe); *Wendy & Peter Pan* (RSC); *The Vortex* (Rose, Kingston); *The Tempest* (Watermill); *Miss Julie Mary Barton, The Way of the World* (Manchester Royal Exchange); *Women Beware Women, The Five Wives of Maurice Pinder, Thérèse Raquin, Pillars of the Community* (National Theatre); *Novecento* (Donmar Warehouse); *A Midsummer Night's Dream* (Regent's Park); *A Number* (Menier Chocolate Factory/Fugard, South Africa); *Mr Kolpert, Where Do We Live* (Royal Court); *The Talented Mr Ripley* (Royal & Derngate); *Much Ado About Nothing* (RSC/Novello); *Thyestes* (RSC/The Other Place); *She Stoops to Conquer* (Birmingham Rep); *The Member of the Wedding* (Young Vic); *Ghosts, The Three Birds* (Gate); *Things of Dry Hours* (Gate/Manchester Royal Exchange); *Love & Money* (Young Vic/Manchester Royal Exchange); *Hamlet* (ETT/West End); *Gone to Earth* (Shared Experience); *King Lear* (Old Vic/ETT), *Bones* (Live/Hampstead); *Lifegame* (Improbable).

Film and television credits include: *Flight, Frayed, No Ball Games, The Life and Times of Vivienne Vyle, French and Saunders, Inside the Mind of Hitler* (BBC); *Heavenly* (Wright/Aardman).

Radio credits include: *The Song Of Hiawatha, The Midnight Cry of the Deathbird (Nosferatu), Pinnochio, The Wizard of Oz, Caligari, Doctor Faustus* (BBC).

MAX PERRYMENT (Sound Designer)

Max is a composer, musician and sound designer living in London. He has composed music for a range of visual media, TV adverts, theatre and dance. Max is the resident composer for Parrot in the Tank and has an MA in Electroacoustic Composition from City University.

Recent theatre credits include: *Creditors, The Remarkable Case of K., The Surplus* (Young Vic); *Sense of an Ending* (Theatre503); *Three Lions* (St. James's); *Black Dog Gold Fish* (The Vaults).

MATTHEW DEWSBURY (Casting Director)

Matthew is the Casting Assistant at the Royal Shakespeare Company. Prior to that he was the Casting and Producing Assistant at the Watermill Theatre.

Credits as Casting Director include: *And Then Come The Nightjars*, *Valhalla*, *Animals* and *A Handful of Stars* – Theatre503/Trafalgar Studios, West End transfer (all for Theatre503); *A Mad World, My Masters* (RSC/ETT); *Little Malcolm and his Struggle against the Eunuchs* (Soggy Arts at Southwark Playhouse); *The Late Henry Moss* (W14 Productions at Southwark Playhouse); *Much Ado About Nothing, Reading Between the Lines*; *Ragnorak* (Eastern Angles).

REBECCA LOUDON (Assistant Director)

Rebecca graduated from the BA Acting Course at Mountview Academy of Theatre Arts and was formerly Artistic Associate of theatre company Custom/Practice.

Directing credits include: *Nights* (White Bear); *Holy Joe* (Rapid Write Response/Theatre503); *A Midsummer Night's Dream* (Brighton Fringe Festival).

Assistant directing credits include: *I and The Village* (Theatre503).

HEATHER DOOLE (Production Manager)

Heather is a freelance production manager. She has previously worked at Theatre503 on *Cinderella and the Beanstalk* and *Animals*.

Other credits include: *State Red, Elephants, Deposit, Deluge, Sunspots* and *36 Phone Calls* (Hampstead Theatre Studio); *Radiant Vermin* (Soho and Tobacco Factory, Bristol); *Albert Herring* (Upstairs at the Gatehouse). She also assisted on *Bull* (Young Vic).

LISA COCHRANE (Stage Manager – London)

Lisa is a freelance stage manager based in London. Originally from Northern Ireland, Lisa found her way across the Irish Sea and completed her drama school training in Professional Production Skills at Guildford School of Acting.

Recent theatre credits include: Assistant Stage Manager on *Don Pasquale/ Rigoletto* (Longborough Festival Opera); Deputy Stage Manager on *A Matter of Life and Death* (Electric Theatre); Stage Manager on *WINK* (Theatre503); Deputy Stage Manager on *Sleeping Beauty* (Blackpool Grand); Stage Manager on Book, *Land of Our Fathers* (Trafalgar Studios); Stage Manager show cover *Richard III* (St Paul's Church); Deputy Stage Manager *King Lear* (Cockpit); Stage Manager on Book *Flesh&Blood Women* (Baby Grand Belfast & tour); Production Manager on *The Kitchen, The Bedroom, and the Grave* (Baby Grand & tour).

BENEDICT JONES (Stage Manager – Bristol)

Benedict trained in Stage Management at the Bristol Old Vic Theatre School and has worked as a stage manager in theatres across the country. He also works as a production manager for Blue Crate Theatre.

Theatre credits include: Company Stage Manager for *Faust* (national tour); Stage and Technical Manager for *Close to You* (Southwark Playhouse/ Brighton Fringe) and *Three Witches* (Belgrade Theatre); Stage Manager for the *GB Theatre Open-Air Shakespeare Tour 2015* (nationwide); *Animals* (Theatre503); the theatre/circus spectacular *Walking the Chains* (The Passenger Shed, Bristol); *Stardust* (South West tour); the *GB Theatre Open-Air Shakespeare Tour 2014* (nationwide); *Spokesong* (Finborough); *Oedipus Retold* (Tristan Bates); *Starry Night – A Nativity Play* (Bristol schools tour); *Moonfleet* (West Country tour); *Surrealissimo, Mr Kolpert* (Alma Tavern); Assistant Stage Manager for *Dancing at Lughnasa* (Tobacco Factory).

JESSICA CAMPBELL (Producer)

Jessica is the Producer and Head of Marketing at Theatre503.

Producing credits include: *Green Living* and *Four Play* (rehearsed readings for the Old Vic); *How I Learned to Drive* and *A Bright Room Called Day* (Southwark Playhouse); *Sense of an Ending* and *A First World Problem* (Theatre503); *Stink Foot* (The Yard Theatre); *Tango* (rehearsed reading for the Young Vic); *Hansel and Gretel* (Bussey Building); *Mephisto* (Oxford Playhouse) and a UK/Japan tour of *The Comedy of Errors* (Southwark Playhouse/Yvonne Arnaud/Stratford's The Dell/Hatfield House/Tokyo Metropolitan Theatre.)

FRANKY GREEN (Associate Producer)

Franky is a freelance theatre producer. She graduated from the BA Drama Course at Bristol University in 2014 and was a Resident Assistant Producer at Theatre503 from December 2014 – June 2015. She is currently an Associate Producer for two theatre companies, Bellow Theatre and Tap Tap Theatre.

Producing credits include: *Billy Through the Window* (Underbelly, Edinburgh Festival/Theatre503); *Captain Morgan and the Sands of Time* (VAULT Festival); *Handmade Tales* (Arcola/London Wonderground Festival/ZOO, Edinburgh Festival); *Men* (Arcola/Underbelly, Edinburgh Festival); *Beautiful Thing* and *Low Tide in Glass Bay* (Alma Tavern, Bristol); *Breathing Corpses* (White Theatre, Bristol); *The Tempest* and *Trash* (Winston Theatre, Bristol).

THANKS

Josephine Baxter
Royce Bell
Annie Brewer at Jerwood Space
Chris Campbell
Philip and Chris Carne
Chris Chapman
Kay Ellen Consolver
Neil Darlison at Arts Council England
Michael Davenport
Joyce D'Silva
Marianne Elliot
Giselle Green
Ben Hall
Hampstead Theatre
Phil and Mandi Heard
Jo Hedley
Henry Hitchings
Dylan Holmes Williams
Polly Ingham
Dennis Kelly
George Linfield
Eleanor Lloyd
Adam Loxley
Marcus Markou
Tanya Ronder
Jack Sain
Geraldine Sharpe-Newton
Jack Tilbury
Erica Whyman
Lily Williams
Roy Williams
Annabel Winder at ETT
The Young Vic

Thanks to the Theatre503 script readers:
Anna Landi, Anna Mors, Ben Hall, Bobby Brook, Brett Westwell, Bridget Hanley, Carla Grauls, Carla Kingham, Claire O'Hara, Corinne Salisbury, Deborah Nash, Deirdre O'Halloran, Jill Segal, Joel Ormsby, Kate Brower, Lisa Carroll, Martin Edwards, Micha Colombo, Sarah Newton, Saul Reid, Tamsin Irwin, Tim Lee, Tom Littler, Tommo Fowler, Vinay Patel, Yasmeen Arden, Catherine Marcus, Kat Andrews, Imogen Sarre, Kealey Ridgen, Kim Marchant, Martha Cooke, Megan Phillips, Sara Gad, Steve Harvey and Zandra Israel.

This production has been supported by:

Theatre503 is the award-winning home of groundbreaking plays.

Led by Artistic Director Paul Robinson, Theatre503 is a flagship fringe venue committed to producing new work that is game-changing, relevant, surprising, mischievous, visually thrilling and theatrical. We are the smallest theatre to win an Olivier award and we offer more opportunities to new writers than anywhere in the UK.

THEATRE503 TEAM

Artistic Director	Paul Robinson
Executive Director	Jeremy Woodhouse
Producer and Head of Marketing	Jessica Campbell
Associate Artistic Director	Lisa Cagnacci
Literary Manager	Steve Harper
Literary Coordinators	Lauretta Barrow, Tom Latter
Office Manager	Emily Hubert
Resident Assistant Producers	Yasmin Joseph, Ceri Lothian, Scott Barnett
'Young Creative Leaders' Project Manager	Louise Abbotts
Volunteer Coordinators	Serafina Cusack, Simon Mander
Associate Directors	Anna Jordan, Jonathan O'Boyle, Tom Littler
Senior Readers	Karis Halsall, Kate Brower, Clare O'Hara, Jimmy Osborne, Imogen Sarre

THEATRE503 BOARD

Royce Bell, Peter Benson, Chris Campbell, Kay Ellen Consolver, Ben Hall, Dennis Kelly, Eleanor Lloyd, Marcus Markou, Geraldine Sharpe-Newton, Jack Tilbury, Erica Whyman (Chair), Roy Williams.

And we couldn't do what we do without our brilliant volunteers
Kelly Agredo, Rosie Akerman, Chidi Chukwu, Rahim Dhanji, Bethany Doherty, Mark Doherty, Fabienne Gould, James Hansen, Tess Hardy, Ken Hawes, Joanna Lallay, George Linfield, Nicole Marie, Charlotte Mulliner, Mike Murgaz, Mandy Nicholls, Annabel Pemberton, Damian Robertson, Larner Taylor, Andrei Vornicu, Danielle Wilson.

Theatre503 is supported by
Philip and Chris Carne, Cas Donald, Gregory Dunlop, Angela Hyde-Courtney and the Audience Club, Stephanie Knauf, Sumintra Latchman, Katherine Malcolm, Georgia Oetker, Francesca Ortona, Geraldine Sharpe-Newton.

Support Theatre503
Help us take risks on new writers and produce the plays other theatres can't, or won't. Together we can discover the writers of tomorrow and produce some of the most exciting plays in the country. With memberships ranging from £23 to £1003 there is a chance to get involved no matter what your budget, to help us remain '*arguably the most important theatre in Britain today*' (*Guardian*).

Benefits range from priority notice of our work and news, access to sold out shows, ticket deals, opportunities to attend parties and peek into rehearsals. Visit theatre503.com or call 020 7978 7040 for more details.

Theatre503, 503 Battersea Park Rd, London SW11 3BW
020 7978 7040 | www.theatre503.com
@Theatre503 | Facebook.com/theatre503

Bristol Old Vic

Bristol Old Vic is the oldest continuously working theatre in the country and will celebrate its 250th birthday in 2016. It enjoys national and international recognition as a theatrical powerhouse, creating ground-breaking theatre whilst nurturing unique and individual talent and serving as a cultural beacon for the city and the South West.

Bristol Old Vic's Literary Department connects with writers across the South West region, offering structured writer development, and identifying production opportunities. We commission new plays and musicals from national and international writers, and advise on adaptations and classics for the Theatre Royal and Studio.

A yearly talent call-out to South West writers takes place each June. Titled 'The Open Session' it invites writers at all levels of experience to send a play or musical for consideration. Scripts are read with the writer's name removed, so anyone can break through based on writing ability, imagination and ideas that inspire.

From these entries, five writers are selected for a year's attachment, receiving dramaturgical support on their current and next play, workshops of drafts to get the work on its feet, use of a quiet writers' room, and the opportunity to be part of the life of our theatre. These writers also become the first we introduce to our creative partners including the BBC, Creative England, Theatre West, and Bristol Old Vic Theatre School.

Our productions have taken our audience on many journeys – from a windswept seaside town in Natalie McGrath's *Coasting* (2011), to a backwoods Cardiff estate in Katherine Chandler's award-winning *Before It Rains* (2012). The compilation evening *Words by Alfred Fagon* (2013) reconnected Bristol to a creative 'lost son' of Jamaica and Bristol. Now Bea Roberts' *And Then Come The Nightjars* (co-presented with Theatre503) tells both a story of enduring friendship and a requiem for rural England.

For more information, visit bristololdvic.org/writers

Bristol Old Vic, King Street, Bristol, BS1 4ED
0117 987 7877 | www.bristololdvic.org.uk
@bristololdvic | Facebook.com/bristol old vic

AND THEN COME THE NIGHTJARS

Bea Roberts

Acknowledgements

Thanks to Sharon Clark for both kicking my arse and holding my hand. A big thank you to Paul, Steve and everyone at Theatre503 for their support and passion.

B.R.

To Mum, Colin, Dad, Linda, Dan and Katy
for the love, patience and Cheesy Bean Crunch

Characters

MICHAEL VALLANCE, *sixty-two to seventy-four, Devonshire accent*
JEFF CRAWFORD, *forty-one to fifty-three, Home Counties accent*

Note on the Text

The play is set between 2001 and 2013.

Action takes place in and around a barn on Michael's farm in the small South Devon village of Ashwalden.

A forward slash (/) indicates the point at which the next speaker interrupts.

A dash (—) denotes a beat or pause.

Punctuation in the script is used to indicate the rhythmic quality of the line.

'MAFF' refers to the Ministry for Agriculture, Farm and Fisheries which became DEFRA in June 2001. When characters talk of MAFF it is pronounced as one word, 'Maff', not spelled out in initials.

'Tavvi' refers to Tavistock.

'Creber's' (in Act Two, Scene One) is pronounced 'Kreeber's'.

This text went to press before the end of rehearsals and so may differ slightly from the play as performed.

ACT ONE

Scene One

2001, Thursday 1st March. Early hours of the morning.

A farm in the heart of the South Devon countryside. A barn; the only point of light and activity in the stillness and quiet of a crisp spring night. We can hear the rustle of straw from a restless cow and, outside, snatches of birdsong. The barn is calm, contented, if a little sleepy.

Sitting in the straw is MICHAEL, *dressed in a muddy navy boiler suit and wellies.*

Sitting by his side is JEFF, *dressed in a wax jacket, cord trousers and wellies.*

MICHAEL *is rolling himself a fag from the tobacco tin and papers on his lap.*

JEFF *is a little drunk and examining his hands. He tries wiggling them and making a fist. His hands are almost numb with cold. He bites the end of one finger to see if it's numb then scrunches up his face at the bitter taste of antiseptic handwash.*

MICHAEL *looks at him;* JEFF *continues pulling a face.*

JEFF. Bleuuugh.

> MICHAEL *hands* JEFF *a hip flask, which he instantly swigs from.*

MICHAEL. Don't put 'em in your mouth then.

—

JEFF. What is known –

MICHAEL. Oh fuck *off*.

JEFF. – what is known as the 'Old Lady of Threadneedle Street'?

—

MICHAEL. You?

JEFF. Capital of Norway.

MICHAEL. Helsinki.

JEFF. Nope. Who / sang –

    MICHAEL *looks at his watch*.

MICHAEL. Half two it's gone now –

JEFF. – 'A Whiter Shade of Pale'?

MICHAEL. – and you're still whinnying on with this stupid fucking quiz.

JEFF. I'm keeping you awake.

MICHAEL. Aren't you just.

JEFF. Come on: 'A Whiter Shade of Pale'.

MICHAEL. It's like being trapped with Michael fucking Aspels.

JEFF. It's fine if you don't know.

    —

MICHAEL. Abba.

JEFF. Abba?!

    —

MICHAEL. I'm gonna put your head through that wall if you're not careful.

    JEFF *sings the first line of 'A Whiter Shade of Pale' by Procol Harum*.

    Chuck you in the slurry pit.

    JEFF *sings the next line*.

    No one would miss you, you know.

JEFF. Doesn't sound a bit like Abba. (*Sings the title of the song.*)

MICHAEL. Such a bender.

Suddenly, the sound of a cow in pain. They stop and stare intently at the cow in front of them.

—

Ah she's grand.

JEFF. Yep.

—

Which author / wrote –

MICHAEL. Jesus fucking wept, Jeffrey.

JEFF. Alright, alright.

MICHAEL. Here's a question – why are you here?

JEFF. You're a miserable sod, you know that?

MICHAEL. Yes.

Come on.

JEFF. What?

MICHAEL. You got a proper tasty bit waiting for you back home in a nice warm bed and yet you been sat here, best part of two hours, boring the arse off me.

JEFF. I have not.

MICHAEL. We had half an hour of who said what at the pub quiz, another half an hour on Mrs Kelly's rabbit's intestines –

JEFF. That was actually fascinating.

MICHAEL. – Holly's grade-three cello, what worktops Helen wants for your new kitchen, I'm surprised you got breath left in you. You better not be fucking billing me.

JEFF. No, your gracious company is thanks enough.

MICHAEL. Tell you, I had your missus waiting in bed I'd be home like a fucking shot, ay?

—

What have you done, Herriot?

JEFF. I haven't – what d'you, why do you assume – don't do a face. No, that's, uncalled for.

MICHAEL. Awwww did I hurt you on your feelings?

JEFF. Yes, I'm going to go and write a *poem*.

—

Thought you might like a hand.

MICHAEL. Jeffrey, how many cattle do you think I've calved in my time?

JEFF. How many?

MICHAEL. I don't fucking know, do I?! Loads. Go home.

—

JEFF. Got a name yet?

—

Arabella? No? Gladys?

MICHAEL. Who'd call a fucking cow Gladys?

JEFF. I would.

MICHAEL. You *would*.

Victoria.

JEFF. Victoria.

MICHAEL. These is the last Sheila named so we got Elizabeth and Anne, Diana, Margaret, Zara, Beatrice, Mary. We lost Camilla to the bloat in February. Who's missing? Ah – Eugenie's with her newborn in the south shed. I'm running out of Royals.

JEFF. Fergie?

MICHAEL *lets out a derisive grunt. Then notices* JEFF *is looking at him and smiling.*

MICHAEL. What's wrong with you?

—

Pardon?

JEFF. It's nice that's all.

MICHAEL. What the bloody hell you supposed to call 'em? Cow One, Cow Two?

JEFF. Alright, alright. If you say so… what about Jeffrey.

MICHAEL. Jesus, can't call a cow Jeffrey. They shouldn't let bloody humans be called Jeffrey.

—

Ever tell you 'bout the time we let Trev name the newborns? He musta been about eight or nine. Sheila's idea o'course, bloody disaster. Tell you, one morning got up and the little buggers'd found an hole in the hedge and there I was, out down them fields in nothin' but boots and 'jamas calling 'Ay, Sheila, I found Bagpuss but there's no sign o' Professor Yaffle.' Well o'course Sam Ellacott across the way hears, so's I walks in to Tavvi market next week, they're all there – / singing the bloody theme tune.

JEFF (*joining in*). – singing the bloody theme tune.

How is Trev?

—

I heard he did all the… arrangements, for the service? Sorted all the flowers and… food –

MICHAEL. Up his street, innit.

MICHAEL *goes to the door and begins to smoke out of the doorway, being careful to fan the smoke so it goes outside.*

The soft purr of a nightjar.

Here's one for you.

—

JEFF. Nightingale?

MICHAEL. Are you special? Nightjar.

JEFF. It's strange.

MICHAEL. You hardly ever see 'em, only hear them. They fly silent. It's bad luck is nightjars. It's a bird o'death.

JEFF (*spooky*). Wooooooooo.

—

MICHAEL. Ellacott's full a shit, in'he? Reckons it's coming
    down this way. That's not why you're here, is it?

JEFF. No.

—

MICHAEL. I don't know how they think they'll close the Moor.

JEFF. Well they have.

MICHAEL. No they *haven't*. How do you 'close' the fucking
    countryside?!

JEFF. Signs? Bits of… tape.

MICHAEL. Oh thank god, well as long as they got bits of tape.

—

    You'd tell me, wouldn't you?

JEFF. It's nowhere near here.

MICHAEL. Mike Leach at Hexworthy just lost his entire herd.
    Everything he had is being piled up and burnt.

JEFF. They're just being… precautions. That's miles.

MICHAEL. Cross your heart?

JEFF. You'll be fine.

MICHAEL. Yeah. Course I fucking will. Nothing wrong with
    my cows.

JEFF. I know.

MICHAEL. You think something's up with Dotty?

JEFF. Jesus Christ, Michael. You'd know if there was.

MICHAEL. Why are you here?

JEFF. Are you kicking me out?

MICHAEL. Yes.

JEFF. Fine.

—

MICHAEL. What the bloody hell is going on, Jeffrey?

JEFF. This is getting really boring.

MICHAEL. Just tell me why you're here then.

JEFF. The scintillating conversation.

MICHAEL. Be serious, Jeffrey.

JEFF. No. No, why is nobody any fun any more?

MICHAEL. Something's up.

JEFF. Alright; I'll play you for it.

MICHAEL. *Fuck's sake*.

JEFF. What's the currency in Japan?

—

Who starred in *Spartacus*?

—

Fine. I'll do a sport one. Which Dutch footballer –

MICHAEL. Ruud Gullit.

JEFF. You didn't hear the –

MICHAEL. Name any other Dutch footballer.

—

Spit it out then.

JEFF. I don't know, I just seem to be a nuisance in my own home these last few months, like a bin bag that keeps wandering back in and sitting on the sofa. Not that I'm allowed to sit on the sofa, or touch the walls – or the floor sometimes – because apparently I live in some terrible DIY battlefield, where everything's always being re-upholstered, or stencilled or shouting at me.

—

Been sleeping in the study on a camp bed for three weeks.
Then every morning I tidy it away so Holly doesn't see and,
we can have the façade of normality. It's constant eggshells.
I'm always in the way somehow and yet when I'm *not* there,
I'm a 'waste of space', apparently, so –

MICHAEL. You *are* a waste of space.

JEFF. Thank you Michael, perhaps you two can form a club.

MICHAEL. You got it made, bey.

JEFF. Oh have I?

MICHAEL. You gotta nice house –

JEFF. Mortgaged up to my arse.

MICHAEL. – lovely looking missus –

JEFF. – with ten different lizard heads, all of which hate me.

MICHAEL. If I had a woman like that bey –

JEFF. Take her! You can have her.

—

Shit. Sorry. Shit. I didn't…

MICHAEL *bats away the suggestion*.

How's… how is it?

MICHAEL. It's the little things that's a bugger, you just catch
yourself. Some mornings I come down and before I know it I
made two cups of tea!

'S funny, was about this time of year. Come back one day
there's a letter, you know, test results, just sitting there
propped up against a pot of daffs. She didn't see out the year.
No fucking age, is it? Fifty-eight?

JEFF. No. It's very cruel.

—

Remember that year, who was it went breach?

MICHAEL. Jojo.

JEFF. Jojo! And we were out here for hours –

MICHAEL. – bloody, pissing icicles!

JEFF. Freezing cold! And when we finally got in to your kitchen, there she was – the magnificent Sheila! Four in the morning, cooking us a fry-up!

MICHAEL. Yeah.

JEFF. I could've kissed her.

MICHAEL. You did kiss her.

JEFF. Oh yeah.

MICHAEL. Yeah. Remind me to knock your block off for that.

Great big heart she had and an arse to match.

JEFF. I should've come to the funeral.

MICHAEL. Don't wanna hear this / again.

JEFF. But I should. Should've come back from Surrey, it's just, Helen and her mother…

MICHAEL. You gotta do for your family. That's how it is.

JEFF. It's got to burst. Whatever this is, this rain cloud hanging over us. We just keep sniping at each other. And circling the plughole.

Christ. I've gone all serious. In which case, it probably *is* time to leave.

MICHAEL. You know your trouble, bey? 'Eat before cider. Or the cider eats you.'

JEFF. A very fine point.

JEFF *goes to leave*.

MICHAEL. Jeffrey. You'd be in charge anyway, wouldn't you? If it comes down here? So you'd make sure it's alright?

JEFF. You're gonna be fine.

MICHAEL. You know you're bloody irritating as hell and you're too fucking cheery and –

JEFF. I'm going, / I'm going.

MICHAEL. No, shut up a minute.

You're the only one I trust with my girls.

JEFF. Nothing's going to happen.

MICHAEL. Swear it –

JEFF *shakes a few drops of tea out of the mugs by their side and pours them each a drink from the hip flask.*

JEFF. Here. To Dotty –

MICHAEL. No, on the newborn.

JEFF. To Dotty and child. May she live long and have gurt big juicy udders, always up for a squeezing!

JEFF *drinks;* MICHAEL *doesn't.*

MICHAEL. No. Do it properly. Properly on it. Go on.

—

JEFF. You want me to go and put my hand on that cow's vulva and swear an oath to you?

MICHAEL. Don't be so fucking crass. Put it on her stomach.

JEFF. Michael –

MICHAEL. Why not?

JEFF. It won't come to that.

MICHAEL. Just – go on, Herriot. Humour an old git.

JEFF *raises his mug.*

It begins to rain.

Scene Two

2001, Monday 7th May.

MICHAEL *has set up camp in the barn. There's a sleeping bag, newspapers, paperwork, dirty cups, a cool box and an old twelve-bore shotgun.*

It's a sombre, misty, grey morning and rain slates down outside the windows. The sound of birdsong has been replaced by the distant whirr of diggers and whinnying of distressed livestock.

MICHAEL *is trying to light a small camping stove with a lighter.*

JEFF *stands by the door in a hazmat suit carrying his vet's bag. He's almost sober.*

MICHAEL. There's one over there, look, by them papers.

JEFF. What?

MICHAEL. Mug, probably need a rinse, mind. Got milk, sugar, the works. Soon as I get this bugger lit.

JEFF. I don't want any tea.

MICHAEL. Even got me little saucepan, look. Egg? I'll do you an egg?

JEFF. No. Thank you.

MICHAEL. Well make yourself at home, 'scuse the mess, butler's on holiday and all that. Ay, tell you what, while I do me gordon blur, where is he, ah –

MICHAEL *finds his baccy tin and holds it out to* JEFF.

– be a good boy, roll us a fag.

JEFF. Michael, you have to unlock the gates.

MICHAEL. Not a fucking chance.

JEFF. They said you threatened to shoot them?

MICHAEL. Just a threat, innit? Come on.

MICHAEL *holds the baccy tin out to* JEFF.

Come on, Herriot. You don't half look a tit you know. Take that stupid jonny off and roll us a fag. I'm gaspin'.

JEFF *stares* MICHAEL *out for a few moments and then reluctantly rolls his suit down to his waist, revealing a shirt and tie. He loosens his tie, sits down and rolls a cigarette.*

What was I doing? Eggs!

JEFF. I'm really not hungry.

MICHAEL. I bet you han't had breakfast, have you? *Have you?*

JEFF. No.

MICHAEL. Well then, you daft sod. 'Go to work on an egg.' That's what they say, d'you remember that one? 'Go to work on an egg.' Clever that. Thinking of getting chickens again. Used to have 'em but it's a bugger keeping the foxes from getting 'em. Come out every morning find there's fucking chicken confetti everywhere.

JEFF *cranes to look out of the barn door. He looks at his watch nervously.*

JEFF. Can you just – come and sit down for a minute please?

MICHAEL. Nice having chickens, innit though, clucking about the place, make it look a bit more *Darling Buds of* fucking *May*, what d'you reckon?

JEFF. Michael.

MICHAEL. What?

JEFF. Are you okay?

MICHAEL (*laughs*). Oh yeah, I am tip-top, bey, top of the pops.

JEFF. You know they're going to start at nine o'clock?

JEFF *holds out the finished cigarette.*

Here.

MICHAEL. Ta.

JEFF. You look shattered.

MICHAEL. Huh. You can talk – state o' you. What you come as? Fucking, attack of the Daleks?

I'll get the water on, do you a dippy egg. You love a dippy egg, don't you, look?

JEFF. I do.

MICHAEL. See!

MICHAEL *starts searching among the papers.*

You got your doodah, mobile? Got the number here somewhere.

JEFF. For MAFF?

MICHAEL *grunts.*

What have they told you?

MICHAEL. Just keep banging on if I don't let the arseholes in I won't get no compensation, but it's not about the fucking money, is it? It's like talking to a brick wall.

JEFF. I've heard the money's… well, it's quite a respectable offer.

MICHAEL. Nah. Got you here now, han' I? You can talk some bloody sense into 'em.

JEFF. I don't know what I could say.

MICHAEL. Just, you done the tests, they'll listen to you, won't they? (*Suddenly furious.*) Oh where the sod is this sodding number?!

JEFF. Look I'll – [find the number.]

MICHAEL. Cheers, mate. Dippy egg yeah?

JEFF. Or a coffee?

—

MICHAEL. Why in fuck would I have fucking coffee out here?! This look like the fucking, Ritz / hotel?

JEFF. Well I don't know what you've got stashed in your cool box!

MICHAEL. You're in a bloody cattle shed, mate.

JEFF. You were going to make tea.

MICHAEL. Yeah *tea*. Tea's normal, innit.

JEFF. *Excuse me*, one minute you're gordon blur doing me a dippy egg and all sorts –

MICHAEL. Do you want a dippy egg?

JEFF. Not really.

MICHAEL. Do you want a cup of tea?

JEFF. No.

MICHAEL. Well off you fuck then!

They laugh. MICHAEL *retrieves a bottle of whisky; he shows it to* JEFF.

Here's a better idea, look. That's your favourite, innit?

JEFF. Thank you.

MICHAEL. Find us some mugs then.

JEFF. Bit early though?

MICHAEL. 'Bit early'? What's got into you?

JEFF. I really shouldn't.

MICHAEL. When've you turned down a free drink?

JEFF. It's not even noon.

MICHAEL. Well drastic times and all that, ay?

MICHAEL *finds two mugs and tips away the slops. He holds them out to* JEFF.

What you waiting for, twelve-gun salute?

JEFF *pours them each a drink.*

There you go, look.

JEFF. What are we drinking to?

MICHAEL. To old friends.

JEFF. Some of us are older than others.

MICHAEL. Sod – [off]

*Suddenly a loud thud as something smacks into the barn
from outside.*

JEFF. Jesus! / What was that?

MICHAEL. Fucking hell!

MICHAEL *jumps up and seizes the gun, he aims it towards
the door.*

JEFF. Michael! Is that loaded?!

MICHAEL *motions for* JEFF *to open the door.*

Can you – *not*? Please?

MICHAEL. Door.

JEFF *opens the door cautiously and exits.*

JEFF *returns carefully holding a stunned baby bird.*

JEFF. Get me that tea towel.

MICHAEL *puts the gun down and spreads a tea towel on the
floor.* JEFF *carefully lays the bird on the tea towel.*

MICHAEL. Poor little bugger. Is he alright?

JEFF. It's breathing, think it's just stunned.

MICHAEL. 'S only a babber an' all.

JEFF. What sort?

–

MICHAEL. It's like trying to teach a dog to drive.

JEFF. *Alright*. What is it?

MICHAEL. Have a guess.

JEFF. Swallow?

MICHAEL. For the cleverest bloke I know, you don't half
know fuck-all. Try again.

JEFF. *Great tit?*

MICHAEL. Only one tit in here. Lapwing.

JEFF. 'Lapwing'.

MICHAEL. It's all this fucking soot and ash what's done it. Poor little fuckers can't see a thing.

Should see the state of our windows. Old Sheils'd go batty she seen what it done to her nets.

JEFF. Yeah, it's been driving Helen mad.

MICHAEL. Can't keep 'em clean?

JEFF. Given up trying. It's the fat rendering down from the pyres, that's where the, all the grease just, coats everything. Holly came in covered, it was all over her bike.

MICHAEL. All this from Ellacott's?

JEFF. Yeah.

MICHAEL. I heard the shots yesterday. That was you?

JEFF *nods*.

His had it?

JEFF. Yep.

—

MICHAEL. How's the babber? He'll be alright, won't he?

JEFF. Yeah I think so, no blood, just needs to recover his senses.

MICHAEL. Dapper little thing, in'he?

JEFF. Mmm, I like his little crest. Very smart.

MICHAEL. Here.

MICHAEL *takes the tea towel with the bird and places it gently out of the way.*

Put him over here, look, so he can see some sun when he wakes up.

JEFF. If we get any sun.

MICHAEL. Don't even seem like spring, does it? So bloody quiet. I an't heard a single bird for weeks, you noticed that?

JEFF. Probably the smoke's upsetting them.

JEFF's mobile phone rings loudly.

Hi.

—

Yep, fine.

—

We're just talking. Can you –

—

No, no, there's no need.

—

I'll call you back.

JEFF hangs up.

MICHAEL. That your little friends, is it?

JEFF. They're not my friends.

MICHAEL. We should get on 'stead of sitting here gossiping like a pair of old biddies. You find that number?

JEFF. You know it's nearly nine o'clock, Michael.

MICHAEL hands a newspaper to JEFF and jabs at an article.

MICHAEL. You seen this? Cumbria. Barricaded the whole farm up! That'd fucking show 'em.

JEFF. I'm going to have to go and let them in.

—

MICHAEL. You what?

JEFF. I tried to say.

MICHAEL. Don't be daft, we're gonna get all this sorted.

JEFF. This is national policy, it's coming *from* MAFF…

MICHAEL. You know the right things to say.

JEFF. It doesn't work like that.

MICHAEL. But it… this, what's happening's all on account a' Ellacott's herd, just cos we share the hedge by the stream but there's no cows in that field. Hasn't been for months. That can't be right, can it? Besides, you tested all my girls yourself, didn't you?

JEFF. Please be reasonable, / Michael.

MICHAEL. All them tests come back negative. Right?

JEFF. Yes but –

MICHAEL. Then why? Why have I got this, this, fucking shitty little bit o' paper, telling me that every living thing within two mile is gonna be slaughtered? You tell me that.

JEFF. The orders from the top are, it has to be / contained.

MICHAEL. 'Orders from the top' what, you gonna start fucking goose-stepping round the yard / in a minute an' all?!

JEFF. It's out of my hands, / Michael.

MICHAEL. Out of your hands?! But you know me, Jeffrey. I've had the disinfectant baths out for weeks and the mats, washed the gates, wheels on all the tractors and trucks. You could eat your dinner off them fence posts amount of time I scrubbed 'em! They're not ill.

JEFF. No.

MICHAEL. So we'll tell them.

JEFF. It doesn't matter.

MICHAEL. No! They can't just waltz in here and do what they like.

JEFF. Yes they can! That's exactly what they can do! Have you actually read any of this?! They've called out the bloody army.

MICHAEL. But this is my farm.

JEFF. I'm sorry.

—

MICHAEL. Come on, bey. This don't make no sense, look. Get
  your mobile.

MICHAEL *lunges at* JEFF *and grabs his phone.*

JEFF. Hey! Christ alive.

MICHAEL *dials.*

You waving a gun about isn't going to stop them, Michael.
  They'll just arrest you and go ahead anyway. Will you listen?

MICHAEL. You can tell 'em we done all the tests. There int
  nothing wrong with any one of my girls. They're not fucking
  setting foot –

Hello, I have to speak to someone immediately.

—

Michael Vallance, Ashwalden.

—

Look, I got the head vet here he wants to speak to someone
  urgent.

—

Dr Jeffrey Crawford. He can tell you hisself. Hang on.

He holds out the phone to JEFF.

(*Into the phone.*) Hang on a minute alright, he's just coming.

Come on then.

Talk to them.

JEFF *doesn't move. He gestures 'There's nothing I can do'.*
MICHAEL *hurls the phone across the barn.*

Fuck's sake! You're not even gonna try, are you?

—

JEFF. Do you think I want to do / this?!

MICHAEL. You're not even gonna try. And you swore to me,
Jeffrey, you *swore*.

JEFF. I haven't got a choice.

MICHAEL. Bollocks have you!

JEFF. The government have decided –

MICHAEL. Oh have they?! You go on then, trot along, like a
good little boy, taking / orders –

JEFF. Oh shut up, Michael! You have absolutely no idea what
you're talking about.

MICHAEL. Don't I?!

JEFF. No. You don't. Trust me. You haven't been outside for
weeks but… I have never seen anything like it – it's like a
war. Day after day there's more rings on the map – it's just
bleeding across the countryside and *I* can't stop it, *they* can't
contain it, it's just fucking everywhere and the more
desperate they get – they're just sending anyone.

–

Last week the slaughter team in Mortenhampstead spooked
the herd so badly they started trying to jump the hedges. I
spent hours rounding them up and then, and then by the time
I got back they'd already built the pyre. And you could hear
that not all those cows were dead. They hadn't stunned them
properly or, god knows. And I spent as long as I could
checking each body to see if it was – but they lit it anyway.
And it got too hot, to keep trying.

I won't let that happen to you. Please let me do it properly.

MICHAEL. Exactly! They don't know what they're doing but
we do. You and me. We hold our ground and we fucking
show 'em that *we know* what's best. Those girls aren't sick,
we got proof. And you and me, bey, right, we'll Butch and
Sundance the lot of them, yeah?! They won't know what's
hit 'em!

JEFF. No.

MICHAEL. 'No'?

—

Fucking, 'no'?!

JEFF. If I don't do it, Michael, they'll just hire in someone else.

—

MICHAEL. Huh. Work's picked up for you something chronic, 'an it?

JEFF. How can you think that?

MICHAEL. Pays well, does it? You know I was wondering about you, cos you never could stand the grizzly bits, could ya? Well buy Helen a few more fucking granite worktops, won't it? Back in the good books now, are we? Yep, plenty o' work for you now.

JEFF. God this is bloody typical of you.

MICHAEL. Well that's all it is, whatever they're paying you I'll double it. Alright?

—

No? Well maybe you want another drink, do you, Jeffrey, before you go out there, go on, steady your nerves. I'll top it up for you, look. Here we are, nice big drink a' whisky for you.

MICHAEL *begins to pour whisky into* JEFF*'s mug until it is overflowing*.

JEFF. Stop it. Stop it!

I *asked* to come here, Michael. I insisted they put me in charge of this job, so I could do my best for you.

JEFF *begins to zip his hazmat suit up*.

MICHAEL. No. I don't believe you. You haven't got it in you, Jeffrey, it's not – Oi!

MICHAEL *grabs* JEFF *by the arm*.

You look me in the eye and tell me what you're going to do my girls. Come on, Dr Crawford. You're going to go into the south shed, you're going to take the newborn off of Dotty, little Victoria. And the second you try that Dotty'll start kicking off so you'll have to get someone to bolt the shed up. You'll take little Victoria outside, her legs is still a bit unstable and she'll be scared an' all, so you might have to carry her. And then what?

JEFF. She'll be stunned with a bolt gun.

MICHAEL. That it? Come on, Jeffrey.

JEFF. I'll shoot her with the bolt gun, here – (*Taps his forehead.*) make sure that the bolt penetrates her frontal cortex and then I'll push a plastic rod into the hole, into her brain and down into her spinal cord to make sure that she's dead.

MICHAEL. And then you'll sling her on a pile and burn her.

JEFF. Yes.

—

A knock at the door.

MICHAEL *seizes his gun and aims it at the door.*

JEFF *stands up in the way of the door.*

MICHAEL (*calls*). You get back on the other / side of that gate!

JEFF. Calm down. (*Calls.*) Everything's fine.

MICHAEL (*calls*). You get off my farm or I'll blow your bloody head off!

JEFF. Calm down. (*Calls.*) Don't move, I'm coming out.

Michael, please just…

JEFF *backs slowly towards the door, he opens it and exits.*

MICHAEL *is left holding the gun aimed at the door. His hands are shaking and he lowers the gun for a few moments.*

MICHAEL *doesn't know what to do with himself.*

The door opens and MICHAEL *hastily aims the gun at the door again.*

JEFF *enters.*

MICHAEL. You told 'em.

JEFF. They've called the police. Michael, stop this. Now.

MICHAEL. *You* stop this.

MICHAEL *moves towards* JEFF *with the gun.*

JEFF. Let me help you.

MICHAEL. Help?! You won't do nothing!

JEFF. There's nothing I can do!

MICHAEL. You spineless, gutless, you're a worm of a man, you know that? Fucking, waste of space! Waste of time I had bothering with you!

JEFF. Come on. Put it down.

MICHAEL. Why?! Why shouldn't I? Do everyone a favour!

—

MICHAEL *begins to cry.*

You're not worth it. You're just a coward. Ten a penny.

MICHAEL *lowers the gun and sits down.*

JEFF *watches him for a few moments and then sits next to him.*

Please, Jeffrey. Nothing's making any sense. No one'll listen to me. Please don't let them take my girls.

JEFF *hesitates and then takes a big drink from the whisky bottle.*

JEFF. I'm sorry.

MICHAEL *gets up.*

MICHAEL. No, just wait, hang on, just wait a minute.

MICHAEL *gets an old cardboard box and starts pulling out rosettes and certificates.*

Breed and Female Champion, Devon County Show, 1994. That one's Dotty's. First, First, Best in Show. Want you to show 'em these. Best Heifer in Milk 1956, that was my Dad's Lillibett, look. '78, Breed Champion '82, '86 that was Lily, Champion Dairy Pair '95, that was Amy and Jojo, '95's when your Holly fell in love with that bay foal and she begged and begged us till we bought it back from the show, what was he called?

JEFF. Chamomile.

MICHAEL. Chamomile. That's it. I let you keep him in my bottom field, took you all year to pay me back but I never said a word to no one. Look at this fucking, Dairy Produce Sculpture 1992, runner-up, Sheils made that horrible angel thing out of butter and it half melted by the time we got there, she did her nut! And you won that stupid bloody pink balloon hat, wouldn't take it off all day. D'you remember that, Jeffrey?

JEFF. I remember.

MICHAEL. They're my girls. That's all I got.

A shot is fired outside. It echoes across the farm.

MICHAEL *and* JEFF *are frozen for a minute and then* MICHAEL *bolts for the door followed by* JEFF.

They exit, leaving the door flapping open.

JEFF (*off*). Michael!

We can hear the sound of rain and anxious cows wailing outside.

Men's voices rise indistinctly from the distance.

Another shot is fired.

MICHAEL (*off*). No!

The rain and the lowing cattle noises continue.

A shot.

—

Another shot.

Something like 'On Hearing the First Cuckoo in Spring' begins to play softly against the noise as MICHAEL*'s cattle are gradually shot one by one.*

Smoke from the pyres begins to fill the stage until it is almost dreamlike.

MICHAEL *emerges from the smoke followed, some way behind him, by* JEFF.

They stand and look out centre stage on a huge smoking pyre of MICHAEL*'s cattle.*

Black charred ash begins to rain gently down in front of them.

The men look on helplessly.

The lights begin to dim.

JEFF *turns and exits, leaving* MICHAEL *standing alone centre stage.*

The lights linger on MICHAEL.

Eventually they fade to a blackout.

End of Act One.

ACT TWO

Scene One

2001, Friday 21st December. Seven months later.

Night. Total darkness. The occasional rustle of the wind through leafless trees. The old barn creaks. MICHAEL *enters from outside with a torch. The torch beam sweeps around the barn.*

MICHAEL. Hello?

I saw someone come in here.

—

His torch light sweeps nervously around the barn.

I got my shotgun so don't go playing silly beggars. Ay?

—

Just ghosts, is it?

Well that's about right.

Hello?

MICHAEL *walks cautiously around the barn, sweeping the beam of the torch. The torchlight shows feet under a tarpaulin.*

Oi.

MICHAEL *walks towards the tarpaulin and kicks the feet.*

Oi! I'm warning you.

Hello?

MICHAEL *pulls back the tarpaulin. It's* JEFF; *he's debilitatingly drunk.*

JEFF. Ugh.

MICHAEL. Jesus, you scared the…

MICHAEL *exits*.

In the darkness we hear boxes shifting and the metallic clunk of tools as he searches for something.

After a few moments, he returns with a lit lantern. He keeps his distance from JEFF *who remains lying down.*

This a joke or something? What do you want?

You're not welcome here, you're not… (*Suddenly angry.*) I should blow your fucking head off!

JEFF. Please do.

MICHAEL. Shut up.

JEFF. Blow my head off!

MICHAEL. Shut up talking stupid things.

She finally kicked you out, has she? God knows you been asking for it.

Why d'you come here?

—

Jeffrey! Why d'you come back here?

JEFF. Used to be warmer.

MICHAEL. 'Used to be warmer.' Yeah did, didn't it. Twenty-two in this shed, nice and toasty it was then wannit, bey? When it was full of cows – d'you remember that, Jeffrey? Been cattle on this land for nearly two hundred years. Then it was all gone. In about an hour.

Ay?

—

Meant to tell you – funny thing happened – Zara's guts burst all across the yard. Just fucking everywhere with flies and maggots, cos your little friends didn't see fit to fucking clear up after theirselves. Just left my girls out there in a great heap. Rained on 'em. Then the sun came out and made 'em steam. Then the smell got so bad you could smell it all across the house, no escaping it there wan't. Imagine if old Sheils had seen that, had to look at that outside her house. So halle-fucking-lujah, ay? Innit grand I'm the only poor bastard left round here for miles.

MICHAEL *kicks* JEFF*'s feet hard.*

Get out, go on! How dare you come here!

JEFF *attempts to get up unsteadily.*

JEFF. I'm going.

MICHAEL. You bastard! You get out now! Go on.

MICHAEL *watches as* JEFF *struggles unsteadily to his feet clutching his head. It takes him several attempts to stand.*

Jesus. I'd heard you were bad but fuck me.

What have you –

MICHAEL *points the lantern at* JEFF*; he grabs* JEFF*'s chin so he can examine his head. There's a lot of blood.* JEFF *flinches and sits back down.*

What have you done?

This all yours?

JEFF. I crashed.

MICHAEL. You fucking idiot! You alright? You broken anything?

MICHAEL *starts manhandling* JEFF *roughly and studying him with the lantern.* MICHAEL *examines* JEFF*'s legs, his arms, his hands.*

JEFF. The windscreen's broken.

MICHAEL. Fuck the windscreen.

JEFF. I think it might be a write-off.

MICHAEL. Where'd it happen?

JEFF. Creber's Lane, Creber's / Lane.

MICHAEL. And you didn't hit no one?

JEFF. No!

JEFF *lies down.*

MICHAEL. Ay, ay. Sit up. Jeffrey.

MICHAEL *pulls* JEFF *up.* JEFF *is very unsteady on his feet and feebly bats* MICHAEL *away.*

JEFF. Get off.

MICHAEL. Alright!

Look, you can sit down but you gotta stay awake.

JEFF. It's late.

MICHAEL. Yeah and you probably got concussion.

Fucking state o' you, Jeffrey. State of all this.

MICHAEL *finds a hanky and starts cleaning the blood off* JEFF*'s head.* JEFF *keeps trying to bat* MICHAEL *away but* MICHAEL *holds* JEFF*'s hands down and continues.*

JEFF. 'Jeffrey, you're a useless bastard.'

MICHAEL. You *are* a useless bastard.

JEFF. 'Fucking waste of space you are, Herriot. You're no good to man nor beast. I should do everyone a bloody favour!'

—

MICHAEL. What the hell were you thinking?

JEFF. I have to go to Dorking.

MICHAEL. *Dorking?* Where the bloody hell is Dorking?

JEFF. Surrey. She's taken Holly, gone to her mother's. I'm not even going to see her on Christmas. She's *my* daughter.

MICHAEL. Shut up feeling sorry for yourself. I don't wanna hear it.

MICHAEL *paces then sits some distance from* JEFF *and starts rolling a cigarette.*

The cold wind whistles around the barn. JEFF *shivers.*

MICHAEL *gets up, strides across the barn. He throws down a battered old blanket beside* JEFF. MICHAEL *sits back down.* JEFF *wraps the blanket around himself.*

JEFF. Smells.

MICHAEL. For the newborns, innit.

JEFF *chucks the blanket down and gets up unsteadily.*

Fuck you doing?

JEFF. I smell.

MICHAEL. Yeah you do smell as it happens, smell to high heaven like a fucking brewery.

JEFF. Nobody wants me here.

MICHAEL. What d'you expect?! Should leave you here to rot.

JEFF. Go on then.

MICHAEL. You what?

JEFF. Fuck off! Fuck off! Leave me here to rot! Go on!

MICHAEL. That's as good as you deserve! Don't see you kipping in Ellacott's barn, ay? He wouldn't piss on you if you were on fire! Nah, only bastard stupid enough to fucking bother with you and where'd that get me, ay?

JEFF *heads for the door.*

Where are you going?

JEFF. Going away.

MICHAEL. How far d'you think you'll get, ay? This weather? Pitch black? Find you dead in a field come morning.

JEFF. Good.

MICHAEL. Oh grow up, Jeffrey! You're bleeding, you fucking idiot. Sit down.

—

Fine, what do I care? Off you pop. Good fucking riddance.

—

Don't you dare come back here.

JEFF *falters*.

Fuck's sake, Jeffrey!

MICHAEL *goes to* JEFF *to support him.* JEFF *pushes* MICHAEL *away.*

JEFF. Get off!

MICHAEL. I'm trying to help you – you baby!

JEFF. Leave me alone.

MICHAEL. This is you all over this is. What, you sad no one likes you no more? Poor Jeff. Boohoo. Boo-fucking-hoo!

You know when you first got here, everyone fucking took to you, didn't they? After five minutes, PTA, pub quiz, fun run, fucking nice house, beautiful little girl –

JEFF. Well I've got fuck-all now! She's selling the house! No wife, no girl, no car – well a car with a lot of tree in it. More tree in it than it's supposed to have.

I'm suspended. '*Compassionate leave*.'

And I am a social pariah.

MICHAEL. You're a whinging fucking bastard and all.

JEFF *laughs*.

I'm not laughing.

—

JEFF. How are you?

—

Are you keeping well?

MICHAEL. You fucking joking?

JEFF. No.

—

I've been having a little trouble, Michael. With everything. Sorry. I'm sorry to disturb your evening.

MICHAEL. Sit down.

—

JEFF. It's cold.

MICHAEL. Yep. Duck pond's frozen. Lucky there int no ducks in it.

—

JEFF*'s head begins to loll as he loses consciousness.*

Ay!

MICHAEL *claps.*

Ay!

MICHAEL *claps in* JEFF*'s face and sits by him.* JEFF *wakes up.*

Wakey wakey.

What's the capital of Sweden? Jeffrey?

JEFF. Oslo.

MICHAEL. Who sang… I don't know, something…

JEFF. Lulu.

MICHAEL. Yep very good. Who wrote *War and Peace*?

JEFF. Lulu.

MICHAEL. Did she. Fuck me.

JEFF. I hated it, you know. I had to do such horrible / things –

MICHAEL. Don't wanna hear it.

JEFF. – and I'm sorry.

MICHAEL. Who won Euro –

JEFF. Michael, I'm so sorry about it all.

MICHAEL. Who won Euro '88?

—

You was always shit at the sports ones.

JEFF. I feel sick.

MICHAEL. When was the last time you actually ate something? D'you even know?

—

Jesus.

MICHAEL *wrestles for some moments with a decision. Then finally fishes in his pocket and retrieves a half-empty packet of crisps, which he holds out to* JEFF.

Here.

—

Have one then. They're beef flavour so it's a bit like dinner.

JEFF *takes a crisp and eats it.* MICHAEL *takes one too. They eat in silence.*

I haven't got much else in.

Sheila'd give me a right ticking-off just having crisps for me dinner. God, she was here she'd go ballistic at the state o' you. She'd bloody drag you in the house shouting her head off, shove you in a hot bath, probably give you a loada my clothes.

You know we was in Tavvi once, saw a wino wearing my tweed jacket. 'Charity begins at home' she says.

She was a wonderful woman.

JEFF. She was.

In the distance, the sound of church bells pealing.

MICHAEL. That's the church kicking out. Should've gone really. Carol singing's the only good bit, innit?

JEFF. Oranges with the candle.

MICHAEL. Yeah, I do like the oranges with the candle. Watch the kids from St Mary's fucking up their lines in the Nativity.

—

JEFF. D'you remember when you were Father Christmas?

MICHAEL. Huh.

JEFF. Sitting in your grotto in the school hall.

MICHAEL. Don't push your luck.

JEFF *touches his head wound*. MICHAEL *knocks his hand away*.

Don't poke it. Fuck's sake.

JEFF. Holly worked it out.

MICHAEL. What?

JEFF. It's your voice. She said why would Father Christmas have a Devon accent?

MICHAEL. Fair point.

JEFF. What was the song? 'You boys and girls won't get any toys!' That one.

MICHAEL. 'Santa Got Stuck Up the / Chimney'.

JEFF. 'When Santa Got Stuck Up the Chimney'! (*Sings*.) 'He began to shout "you boys and girls" – '

MICHAEL. '"You girls and boys" – '

JEFF. Go on.

MICHAEL. *Fuck off*.

—

MICHAEL *sighs*.

I don't remember it.

JEFF. Balls.

MICHAEL. 'When Santa got stuck up' –

JEFF. With the actions.

MICHAEL. Do you want me to do it or not?

JEFF. Sorry.

The lights fade slowly.

MICHAEL (*sings softly*). 'When Santa got stuck up the chimney, he began to shout "You girls and boys won't get any toys if you don't help me out. My beard is black, there's soot in my sack, my nose is tickly too." When Santa got stuck up the chimney – "Achoo, achoo, achoo".'

–

JEFF. Can I come in the house?

MICHAEL. I don't know yet.

The church clock strikes.

End of Act Two.

ACT THREE

Scene One

2011, August. Eight years later.

Darkness.

The first upbeat chords of Maroon 5's 'Moves Like Jagger'. The pulsing beat comes in.

A brilliant flash as many coloured disco lights criss cross, weave and dance across the stage.

A spurt from a disco smoke-machine.

Holly's wedding reception. Late night.

JEFF *(fifty-one) and* MICHAEL *(seventy-two) appear dancing in their best suits.*

JEFF *has got rhythm and some slick moves.* MICHAEL *is fairly drunk and a little unsure of how to dance to this music but has a good stab at it.*

JEFF *dances in a Mick Jagger impression.* MICHAEL *laughs.*

JEFF *tries to show* MICHAEL *some dance moves.* MICHAEL *attempts to copy him.* JEFF *shows him again.* MICHAEL *still can't get it.*

MICHAEL *starts to take the piss out of how* JEFF *was dancing, gesturing with a limp wrist that* JEFF *is camp.* JEFF *doesn't care; he's enjoying himself too much dancing.*

Another large spurt of smoke from the smoke machine engulfs MICHAEL.

MICHAEL. Jesus!

> *As the smoke clears we see* MICHAEL *bent double having a coughing fit.* JEFF *stops dancing and helps* MICHAEL *to a straw bale in the corner.* MICHAEL *sits.*

JEFF *exits.* MICHAEL *wipes his sweaty forehead. He's out of shape, growing more frail, he looks bewildered.*

JEFF *returns with a glass of water which he gives to* MICHAEL. MICHAEL *gratefully drinks.*

JEFF. I said we shouldn't hire Dodgy Dave.

MICHAEL. David is the finest disc jockey this side of Exeter.

JEFF. He's cheap you mean.

MICHAEL. That's by the by.

JEFF. He works on the Waltzers.

MICHAEL. Oh sorry, *Princess Margaret.* Holly's having a blinding time though, look?

JEFF. Yeah.

MICHAEL. Gorgeous, in't she?

JEFF. Of course.

MICHAEL. Dun't get that from you. When she walked down that aisle was like an angel walked in the room. Made my heart stop. You should be proud o' your girl.

JEFF. I really am.

MICHAEL. You should be. Shame old Sheils ain't here, she bloody loved a wedding. Bloody loved a buffet 'n'all. Speaking of –

– what the fuck's he doing here?

JEFF. Who?

MICHAEL. Fucking Ellacott.

JEFF. Leave it.

MICHAEL. Not enough he's fucking selling up to the highest bidder now he's got his snout in my buffet! Bloody shameless bastard.

JEFF. Not now.

MICHAEL. Oh come on, you gotta have a fight at a wedding, it's tradition! Give that lot something to gawp at. God, Helen's new bit's a jumped-up tosser, in'he?

JEFF. He's an estate agent.

MICHAEL. Course he fucking is!

JEFF. Apparently they're 'considering taking the plunge' .

MICHAEL. Ah sod 'em. You're best off out of it, mate. She han't half got an arse on her these days.

JEFF. She has stacked it on since the divorce.

MICHAEL. 'Mother of the Bride', more like, fucking, Free Willy!

This is nice, innit. Barn's scrubbed up well.

JEFF. Yeah, who would have thought.

MICHAEL. Good on you, bey, not letting that batch a' bastards upset you, like bloody, mother-in-law, HMS Pinafore over there.

JEFF. Barbara? Old Barbara's been having a field day. 'Orange juice, is it, Jeffrey? Well that does make a change!' She never did like me.

MICHAEL. She's another one fucking boring as sin, lording it over everyone with her too-much perfume and her, what's it? – Plumes. I said to her 'What you come as, love – Admiral Nelson?'

JEFF. You didn't say that?

MICHAEL. I did.

JEFF. Ha! Well, good. Bollocks to her.

MICHAEL. Bollocks to her indeed! Never had to do an ounce of all that whatnot you did, don't know nothing about fucking willpower or change – see, bey, she was born a posh old twat and she'll die the same and all! In't no twelve steps for that!

Anyway, bloody lord of the manor now, int you.

JEFF. Hardly.

MICHAEL. We done alright. We'll double the herd by next year. Fix the roof, go organic, get a hot tub!

JEFF (*joining in*). – go organic, get a hot tub. Yeah, I know.

MICHAEL. Look at him. Greedy bastard with his cheeks full of my teriyaki skewers. Can buy his own now, can't he? He can fucking afford it.

JEFF. You can't blame him.

MICHAEL. And where's it leave the rest of us? Fucking houses everywhere? Wake up one morning, go for a piss there'll be a fucking Tescos opened up in me toilet.

—

JEFF. I was talking to my cousin Steve earlier.

MICHAEL. Oh yeah?

JEFF. He's doing really well.

MICHAEL. Bald bloke? Looks like that one I hate off the, thing.

JEFF. No that's Terry, Steve's – look – talking to Pippa, with the green dress.

MICHAEL. Oh she is a lovely woman.

JEFF. Anyway, Steve / reckons –

MICHAEL. I said to her 'You got a look of Gina Lollobrigida, you. You ever hear that, sweetheart?'

JEFF. Listen –

MICHAEL. Gina Lollobrigida. Fuck me, they don't make 'em like that any more, bey. You think they'd get to a certain size and she wouldn't keep her balance no more. Remarkable. See, Sheila had a good pair on her but then she had the backside to, you know, act like a counterbalance, sort of thing.

JEFF. Michael?

MICHAEL. What?

JEFF. Steve's in property, he said land prices round here are really shooting up. I mean, look at this place.

MICHAEL. The barn?

JEFF. You know *Grand Designs*?

MICHAEL. I fucking hate *Grand Designs*.

JEFF. I know –

MICHAEL. How is it always fucking on? Night and day. It's all they ever show, have its own bleeding channel soon.

JEFF. Listen, we could do a conversion – holiday lets, conferences, weddings.

MICHAEL. We're already having a wedding.

JEFF. Exactly!

—

Don't worry about it.

—

Forget it, we'll talk about it tomorrow.

MICHAEL. We're not having *Grand Designs* round here, fucking putting bidets left right and centre!

JEFF. Not actually *Grand Designs*. It doesn't matter.

MICHAEL. Why are you always fiddling with the house?

JEFF. I'm not.

MICHAEL. Let you move in out the goodness of my heart and suddenly it's all bloody, 'insulate' that and 'floorboards' this.

JEFF. It's just an idea.

MICHAEL. Where is he? This Steve bloke?

JEFF. It's almost time for the fireworks, look.

MICHAEL. Ay ay ay – what's got into you?

JEFF. This isn't the time. I shouldn't have bought it up.

MICHAEL. What have you said to him?

JEFF. Steve? I said he could come and give us a valuation. It's just an idea! If we convert the barn for holiday lets or conferences or whatever –

MICHAEL. But it's not, is it? It's a cow barn not a spa, not a conference centre, fucking hotel, plot of land. Fucking sick of these people!

JEFF. *Michael*.

MICHAEL. Why can't I have a farm? Why does everyone have to go messing with things, sticking their grubby little fingers into everything? People still gotta eat, don't they? Still gotta grow plants, can't do that in a test tube yet, can you? Can't just get milk out a packet? I don't understand people no more. What were you thinking, Herriot?

JEFF. It's just a way we could stay here and actually make some money. I mean, we're sitting on acres of real estate.

MICHAEL. I'm sitting on my farm. Alright?

JEFF. *Our* farm.

–

MICHAEL. You go and tell that Steve he can fucking whistle for it.

JEFF. I don't know how much longer we can hold out, Michael. You know how it's been. Soon it'll be winter again and we'll be back to living by the Rayburn cos every other room's got damp patches turning to ice, roof leaking – the windows are so creaky they're basically held together with cobwebs. Why not use the barn? Just use some of the land – that's better than having it fall apart? Isn't it?

MICHAEL. Bloody washing and ironing and playing charlady to a loada posh twats –

JEFF. But nothing's *working*. Look, we tried. And we couldn't have done more but Dairycrest's got us by the bollocks –

MICHAEL. What so we just give everything up to people come here treat this whole county like a fucking hotel? Like it's all been put here for their weekend and their postcards. Don't let 'em come here and bully you. Been walking round here. I heard the lot of 'em: 'Oh how lovely. It's like an oil painting' but it's not a painting, is it? It's actually here. It's proper. Ten years ago they would've been ankle-deep in cow shit.

JEFF. And now? We've got maybe a couple of months left.

MICHAEL. We'll double the herd, go organic –

JEFF. With money from what? We're tapped out. (*Gesturing to the party.*) This is the last of it.

—

I don't know what else we can do.

Enjoy the party I suppose.

—

JEFF *looks at his watch. He climbs on a hay bale to make an announcement.*

Ladies and gentlemen, if I could have your attention please? Dave – could you turn the music – thanks. Ladies and gentlemen, the fireworks are due to start any minute! Please make your way outside, sharpish!

JEFF *climbs down.* MICHAEL *doesn't move.*

I'm going outside.

—

Are you coming?

—

The fireworks begin. JEFF *races outside, leaving* MICHAEL *alone on stage.*

Scene Two

2013, October. Two years later. Dusk. The hayloft of the barn.

MICHAEL *sits by a small window wrapped in a duvet. He is dying of emphysema.*

There are mugs, a newspaper and some food wrappers near him; he has obviously been nested for some hours.

Below, JEFF *is attempting to climb the ladder carrying two mugs of tea. He is wearing a ladies' purple padded anorak which is too small for him.*

He scalds himself.

JEFF. Ow! Bollocks.

  MICHAEL *smiles weakly.*

MICHAEL (*calls*). Just carry – (*Coughs.*)

JEFF (*calls*). What?

MICHAEL (*calls*). Just – (*Coughs.*)

JEFF (*calls*). Shut up, you're making yourself cough.

  JEFF *enters with two mugs of tea.*

  Here's your tea sir, just how you like it, strong enough to kill a small pony.

MICHAEL. Old Sheils'd wet her knickers she saw you standing there like that in her coat.

JEFF. Yes, well, someone chucked mine in the slurry pit.

MICHAEL. Did they?

JEFF. Yes they did.

MICHAEL. I imagine you was being a knob.

JEFF. You imagine?

MICHAEL. Probably. Hang about, you're not wearing her knickers too, is you? Is that what's wrong, you got your knickers on too tight? That's it! It's cutting off circulation to your brains?

JEFF. Very droll.

MICHAEL *laughs and starts coughing again.* JEFF *starts going through* MICHAEL*'s pockets.*

MICHAEL. Get off me.

JEFF. Where's your tablets?

MICHAEL. I don't want a tablet.

JEFF. Do you want some water?

MICHAEL. Bollocks to water, you wanna be useful, roll us a fag.

JEFF. Absolutely not.

MICHAEL. What difference it gonna make now, ay? Herriot?

JEFF. I maintain that this is a pissing stupid idea you know

MICHAEL *dismissively waves the suggestion away with his hand.*

MICHAEL. Roll us a fag.

JEFF. You'd be more comfortable in bed.

MICHAEL. Get on, '*bed*'! Best views in Devon here, you see down to the Tamar that way, look, that's Calstock there near them aquaducts, viaducts, whatever them ducts are. God's own country this is, Jeffrey!

Seen this?

JEFF *goes to look out of the window.*

JEFF. Where?

MICHAEL. Diggers. Past the church spire, look.

JEFF. Heard what they're gonna call the new estate? I'm not sure I should tell you actually, it's not good for your blood pressure.

MICHAEL. Oh let me fucking guess – Dingley Nightingale Twinkle fucking Glade?

JEFF. Worse.

MICHAEL. Honeysuckle Badger Sparkly Lane?

JEFF. 'Shepherd's Dell'.

MICHAEL. *'Shepherd's Dell'! Jesus!* Where's me shotgun?
Fucking shoot me in the head now that I live to see
Shepherd's – what the fuck's a 'dell'?!

JEFF. I think it's where pixies live.

MICHAEL. Not pixies! Christ. What is wrong with people?

JEFF. The irony being, the shepherd's working on that building
site.

MICHAEL. Who's that? Shane – whatsit?

JEFF. Shane Dimpsey.

MICHAEL. Dimpsey, is he?

JEFF. Apparently.

MICHAEL. You best keep your distance then.

JEFF. Why?

MICHAEL. Don't remember, do you?

JEFF. Oh God, what?

MICHAEL. Well, back when you was, you know, / being a
drunk wanker –

JEFF. Alcohol dependent.

MICHAEL. – you tried it on with Shane Dimpsey's missus, in
front of everyone – including him – in the beer garden of
The Drake.

JEFF. Is that all?

MICHAEL. Well you didn't have no trousers on at the time, see.

JEFF. I didn't?

MICHAEL. No, you'd chucked up down yourself so you saw fit
to take 'em off and fling 'em in a tree.

JEFF. Shit.

MICHAEL. Ruined their Carly's Sweet Sixteen, that did. He nearly battered you to death in the car park. Still. I laughed.

JEFF. Sorry.

—

MICHAEL. So he's on the building sites now, is he? Shame.

I've changed my mind. I don't wanna be buried in the churchyard no more, I wanna be stuffed and put in that bottom field so I can scare the shit out of everyone in Shepherd's Dell.

JEFF. Or I could bury you with just your arse sticking out?

MICHAEL. Yeah, give you somewhere to park your bike.

JEFF. No, too much work. I'll just sling you in the compost bin. You'll mulch up lovely come spring.

MICHAEL *laughs so hard he has a coughing fit.*

JEFF *searches in the debris.*

I'll get you some more water.

MICHAEL. Tea.

JEFF *checks the tea's not too hot. He hands it to* MICHAEL, *who sips it.*

JEFF. Forgot – I got you a present. We've got loads. We should get them in some vinegar, have a conker tournament.

JEFF *hands* MICHAEL *a spiky, lime-green horse chestnut.* MICHAEL *smells it.*

MICHAEL. Thass a beauty. Look at it. Magnificent, innit, Jeffrey?

JEFF. It is. It's getting dark. We should think about getting you to bed.

MICHAEL. Ah let's stay up a bit longer, ay?

JEFF. You've been up here all day. Besides, dinner'll be ready soon. I've made Cheesy Bean Crunch.

MICHAEL. I hate Cheesy Bean bollocking Crunch.

JEFF. There's protein in beans, they're good for you.

MICHAEL. You'll finish me off with your bloody rabbit food.

—

JEFF. Actually, Michael, rabbits eat their own mucus-covered cecal pellets as they emerge from the anus.

MICHAEL. You're a filthy bastard.

See the lights, look.

JEFF *looks out of the window.*

JEFF. Of course. Goosey Fair Day today, can you believe it, already? Comes around quicker and quicker. Used to take Holly, well, until she got too cool to go with me. Bought her a great big plastic tiara one year, flashing lights on it, she wouldn't take it off. Really annoyed Helen, which was a bonus, of course. She was outraged I'd got her something so '*gaudy*'. But that's the charm of a fair, isn't it? It's sort of, gloriously shit. She always wanted it to be like something out of Jane Austen.

MICHAEL. Trev won a goldfish one year, on the shooting gallery.

JEFF. I don't know how I feel about that.

MICHAEL. Don't worry about them – hard as fucking nails fairground goldfish, could fight a dog. Lived in a vase for the first six months. He had that fish for bloody years, lasted till he went off to college.

JEFF. What was it called?

MICHAEL (*sighs*). 'Marty Maraschino.' She's buried in a matchbox beneath the rowan tree. It's from *Grease*, with the Pink Ladies and that, you ever watch that film?

JEFF. On a loop, Holly loved *Grease*.

MICHAEL. So did Trev.

JEFF. Be good if he came to stay one weekend? I've got his email.

MICHAEL. Yeah. Perhaps.

JEFF *looks pleasantly shocked.*

JEFF. I'll see when he and Jack are free.

MICHAEL *grunts.*

What now for us then? Get the bonfire lit after supper, toast some crumpets? Or have some sort of pagan orgy? I'll ring Mrs Tebbs from the post office, get her to bring her sister Eunice? I hear she'll do anything for a custard slice and a game of bingo.

MICHAEL *starts laughing and coughing again.*

Sorry.

MICHAEL. Can you smell that? Autumn. Smells like smoke and frost and wet moss. Should get that bonfire lit, dry spell won't last.

Sheila'd always make me a blackberry crumble.

JEFF. She was a cracking cook.

MICHAEL. She was.

That's how come she had an arse the size o' Tiverton.

Ay, I been thinking – remember that New Year we come up here, all that fuss she made coming up here in them stilettos?

JEFF. It was alright for you, I was the one holding the ladder. Why wouldn't she put her wellies on?

MICHAEL. Showing off to your Helen, wan't she? Great night that was, sitting up here watching the fireworks.

JEFF. Helen got so pissed she kept calling it 'the min-ellium' Happy Min-ellium!

MICHAEL. Happy Min-ellium.

We had our first fumble in this barn, me and old Sheils. She was bloody gorgeous, love o' my life. Bloody hurry up and find yourself a bird, Jeffrey. You find yourself a good woman and you be happy.

JEFF. I should. God help me. The only fanny I've seen in years is you.

MICHAEL *starts laughing and coughing again.*

MICHAEL. I never moved house. Not once. I ever tell you that?

JEFF. Yes, you did.

MICHAEL. Born upstairs.

JEFF. I didn't know that.

MICHAEL *(nods)*. My mother was back milking the cows within the hour.

We had a good run, didn't we, Jeffrey?

JEFF. You finished your tea?

MICHAEL. Muddled through, han't we?

JEFF. Life of Riley. Telly in the kitchen.

MICHAEL. Telly in the kitchen! Sheila'd never let me have a telly in the kitchen.

JEFF. There you go, some dreams do come true. Come on, it'll be dark soon. My Crunch is gonna burn.

MICHAEL. It's all yours. The house.

JEFF. Gonna be far too cold up here if we don't get a move-on.

MICHAEL. I said the house is yours, Jeffrey.

JEFF. Don't be daft.

MICHAEL. I know I 'an't been the easiest bloke to live with.

JEFF. You're a colossal and perpetual pain in the arse.

MICHAEL. You're a pain in the arse.

JEFF. I am. Come on, it's getting cold.

—

MICHAEL. Lucky bastard really. To have all this. Have a woman like Sheila and, be here, have a life here, never wanted to go anywhere else, you know. Went to Coventry once.

JEFF. Oh yeah?

MICHAEL. It was fucking awful.

JEFF. Yeah.

MICHAEL. You can go anywhere you like though, eh? Jeffrey?
You do that.

JEFF. Don't be such a girl.

MICHAEL looks out of the window.

JEFF pats MICHAEL on the shoulder.

MICHAEL shakily reaches up and squeezes JEFF's hand.

*They sit like that for a few moments, looking out of the
window. The sound of birds at dusk.*

*MICHAEL raises JEFF's hand to his lips; he kisses the back
of JEFF's hand and then pats it brusquely. JEFF's face
flushes and tears prick his eyes. He looks away and pats
MICHAEL's hand back.*

*They stay holding hands and MICHAEL closes his eyes. His
breathing is unsteady and difficult.*

*JEFF watches him anxiously and then stares at the ceiling,
trying desperately not to cry.*

MICHAEL. What's the, what's the longest river in Africa,
Jeffrey?

JEFF. The Nile.

MICHAEL. Is it?

JEFF. You're a terrible quizmaster.

MICHAEL. Mmm.

—

What d'you call a lanky git in a stupid coat?

JEFF. Very good.

MICHAEL. Ay, listen.

They listen to the bird calls at dusk.

Come on, Jeffrey, even you know this one.

JEFF. It's a nightjar.

Something like 'A Whiter Shade of Pale' begins to play softly.

The sun sets.

The autumn winds scatter dead leaves from the branches.

JEFF *and* MICHAEL *sit in silence holding hands.*

Curtain.

Other Titles in this Series

Mike Bartlett
BULL
GAME
AN INTERVENTION
KING CHARLES III

Tom Basden
THE CROCODILE
HOLES
JOSEPH K
THERE IS A WAR

Jez Butterworth
JERUSALEM
JEZ BUTTERWORTH PLAYS: ONE
MOJO
THE NIGHT HERON
PARLOUR SONG
THE RIVER
THE WINTERLING

Caryl Churchill
BLUE HEART
CHURCHILL PLAYS: THREE
CHURCHILL PLAYS: FOUR
CHURCHILL: SHORTS
CLOUD NINE
DING DONG THE WICKED
A DREAM PLAY *after* Strindberg
DRUNK ENOUGH TO SAY
    I LOVE YOU?
FAR AWAY
HOTEL
ICECREAM
LIGHT SHINING IN
    BUCKINGHAMSHIRE
LOVE AND INFORMATION
MAD FOREST
A NUMBER
SEVEN JEWISH CHILDREN
THE SKRIKER
THIS IS A CHAIR
THYESTES *after* Seneca
TRAPS

Fiona Doyle
COOLATULLY
DELUGE

Vivienne Franzmann
MOGADISHU
PESTS
THE WITNESS

debbie tucker green
BORN BAD
DIRTY BUTTERFLY
HANG
NUT
RANDOM
STONING MARY
TRADE & GENERATIONS
TRUTH AND RECONCILIATION

Stacey Gregg
LAGAN
OVERRIDE
PERVE
WHEN COWS GO BOOM

Sam Holcroft
COCKROACH
DANCING BEARS
EDGAR & ANNABEL
PINK
RULES FOR LIVING
THE WARDROBE
WHILE YOU LIE

Vicky Jones
THE ONE

Anna Jordan
CHICKEN SHOP
FREAK
YEN

Lucy Kirkwood
BEAUTY AND THE BEAST
    with Katie Mitchell
BLOODY WIMMIN
CHIMERICA
HEDDA *after* Ibsen
IT FELT EMPTY WHEN THE
    HEART WENT AT FIRST BUT
    IT IS ALRIGHT NOW
NSFW
TINDERBOX

Cordelia Lynn
LELA & CO.

Chloë Moss
CHRISTMAS IS MILES AWAY
HOW LOVE IS SPELT
FATAL LIGHT
THE GATEKEEPER
THE WAY HOME
THIS WIDE NIGHT

Paul Murphy
VALHALLA

Stuart Slade
CANS

Stef Smith
REMOTE
SWALLOW

Jack Thorne
2ND MAY 1997
BUNNY
BURYING YOUR BROTHER IN
    THE PAVEMENT
HOPE
JACK THORNE PLAYS: ONE
LET THE RIGHT ONE IN
    after John Ajvide Lindqvist
MYDIDAE
THE SOLID LIFE OF SUGAR WATER
STACY & FANNY AND FAGGOT
WHEN YOU CURE ME

Phoebe Waller-Bridge
FLEABAG

Tom Wells
JUMPERS FOR GOALPOSTS
THE KITCHEN SINK
ME, AS A PENGUIN

A Nick Hern Book

And Then Come The Nightjars first published in Great Britain in 2015 as a paperback original by Nick Hern Books Limited, The Glasshouse, 49a Goldhawk Road, London W12 8QP, in association with Theatre503, London

And Then Come The Nightjars copyright © 2015 Bea Roberts

Bea Roberts has asserted her right to be identified as the author of this work

Cover image by Adam Loxley

Designed and typeset by Nick Hern Books, London
Printed in the UK by Mimeo Ltd, Huntingdon, Cambridgeshire PE29 6XX

A CIP catalogue record for this book is available from the British Library

ISBN 978 1 84842 511 8